THE POWER OF NLP

Attract More Wealth, Better Health, And Improve Relationships

MATT MORRIS

CONTENTS

Introduction	v
1. How To Build Rapport	1
2. The Body, The Mind, and NLP	7
3. Change Your Emotions with NLP	14
4. Get Healthy With NLP	21
5. Attract More Wealth	24
6. NLP in Business	28
Afterword	35

Introduction

Neuro-linguistic Programming (NLP) is a field of study in Psychology that unlocks human potential by changing the way we see things. It solves our problems by shifting our perspectives so that we can improve our lives (Witkowski, 2010). Then it follows a change in language or replaces a word used in a sentence to completely shift the emotion or feeling produced by the sentence.

Changing how we perceive and identify ideas will change how our mind reacts (or responds). Our brain is programmed to react to various phenomena simply by recalling concepts based on habits, patterns, and strategies. NLP techniques can be used to change these habits to get the results we desire (Dilts, 1980).

Neuro-Linguistic Programming (NLP) was pioneered in the 1970s by a Linguistic specialist named John Grinder and a Gestalt therapist named Richard Brandler. They theorized that our minds are tied closely to our language and behavior.

INTRODUCTION

Their techniques were proven effective against stage fright, phobias and anxiety (Hofmann, 2009). However, NLP is not limited to solving phobias and anxiety. Its biggest use is in the field of interpersonal relationships and communicating more effectively.

NLP has shown people how to adapt to various personality types, creating more rapport, harmony and friendships. It has improved our ability to connect with each other so that we can understand each other at a deeper level. For example, it allows you to adjust the type of language you use in order to connect with that person easier, based on whether the person is a visual, kinesthetic, or auditory learner simply by watching their eye movements (discussed in Chapter 2).

NLP has also shown us that *we* are the biggest solution to any challenge we may be facing. You have the ability to *choose* to let your emotions work for you or against you. Problems are caused by choices and decisions that have already been made, and the right mindset can often relieve them of any disappointment, anger, and stress.

Each person has created their own vision of the world with their five senses. Our senses create a mental map out of the things we see, hear, taste, smell and touch. These mental maps are how we perceive the world. However, this perception doesn't mean it's factual, or the true reality. It is a subjective reality, which is the concept of varying perspectives.

An example of subjective reality is water. Swimmers will think about going towards the sea to enjoy the water. Others will stand in shock over the fear of drowning. Two subjective realities are revealed: water is an enjoyable place and water kills. The contrasting ideas happen because people have different

INTRODUCTION

backgrounds. The person with Hydrophobia possibly had a near-death experience during childhood that carried on towards adulthood. The swimmer on the other hand, might have been taught how to swim at an early age and thus enjoys the sea.

How To Build Rapport

Building friendship, harmony and, most importantly, trust, is the key to flourishing relationships. These are core components to building rapport, which is a sense of acceptance and trust. Having goodwill among each other can make it easier for us to open up, connect and have amazing interactions.

Everybody has their own type of person they naturally click with or prefer to interact. If communication between two people is not in sync, chances are, they won't get along. At the same time, it is still easy to develop a strong relationship or build rapport with that person.

Mirroring

Essentially, mirroring is mimicking the behavior of the person you're talking to. Under the law of attraction, people easily bond with others that exhibit the same trait as they do. First impressions last, which is one of the reasons mirroring is such an important technique when first interacting with someone. Mirroring others makes it easier to understand other people's' energies and build rapport (Clibby, 2004).

Mirroring is done best if it's subtle, as in not copying your subject's every movement from head to toe, but instead taking on or imitating some of the movements of the other person, such as their head position or arm movements. This might feel uncomfortable at first and after doing it a few times you will get comfortable with it and the other person will appreciate it, whether they notice it or not.

1. **Match the body language**

If the person you're talking to has a straight posture, you should match it. If the person has their arms crossed, subtly cross yours. If their head is tilted slightly, tilt yours as well. Return the same gestures like handshakes and smiles to develop courtesy and trust. They will feel appreciated, loved and are more willing to open-up.

1. **Match breathing rhythms**

The rhythm of your breath explains the energy that you are using. Slow breathing is a sign of calm and relaxed energy. While, fast rhythmic breathing indicates an anxious or nervous state. How do you want to come across?

1. **Match the tone of voice, rhythm, and tempo**

Loudness indicates the intensity of emotions. A loud voice is a sign of anger and frustration, whereas a soft but audible one indicates calmness. How do you want to come across?

Pitch is the tone of your voice. A high pitch is perceived as exciting and a low one is associated with anger. It's kind of like a chihuahua serious but informal conversation like a sales talk uses a moderate pitch.

Rate refers to the speed of speaking. A gradual increase in rate signifies a rise in intensity. Too much rate, however, is a sign of nervousness. On the other hand, boredom or disinterest is associated with a slow rate. **Quality** is your key to be understood. Pronunciation, articulation and idiolect (personal manner of speaking) are things you need to keep in mind for effectively communicating.

Silence dictates the flow of your conversation. Match the silence that your partner gives you. Silence gives you the chance to listen and regroup your thoughts.

Caution should be used when mirroring. You don't want to look like a robot or Do not mirror *everything* your subject does in one go. Start with posture then move to body language until you reach the stage of mimicking paralanguage. Whenever your subject does something, return the favor, but this time, make the movement smaller. Rapport is all about matching the energy with the people you are interacting with.

Systemic processes of the environment and mind

Our minds are tightly interconnected with our environment. The various stimuli that we receive from the world are brought to our brains to interpret. Afterwards, our minds create a perception about it - either negative or positive. Therefore, if you place a negative view on the situation, it will remain negative and you will only see the mistakes until you make the conscious effort to find the positives or the things that went *right* about it. These perceptions are what become your reality.

For more information, I highly recommend taking a look at my book titled Positivity, which discusses how to become positive minded.

One small request before we get too much further is that you use the power of NLP with integrity and good judgement, and if you are ever in question whether or not something is appropriate, reach out to a qualified NLP professional.

Filtering

In NLP, it is believed that every behavior has a positive intention(Ellerton, 2013). Although the positive intent may not be clear or even make sense according to someone else's view of the world, for the person engaging in the behavior, it makes sense in their model of the world or their reality. This understanding helps to explain why not everyone wants the same things in life, or reacts in the same way to situations in life. This goes to show that we each have different perceptions - not that one of us right and the other wrong.

Even though you might not agree with another person's' reality, it is important to not judge the person but rather to appreciate and respect that they have different beliefs and values from you. Respect that the other person may hear, see, feel and perceive the world differently than you do. Therefore he won't be driven by the same values, or make the same choices as you.

For example, if you are talking with someone and all of a sudden he raises his voice at you, yells, or disappears into his bedroom, you might find this completely unacceptable behavior. Be curious about it. Take a look at it from his perspective. With his model of the world, and his circumstances in life perhaps he felt uncomfortable or overwhelmed in the conversation and he felt that was the only option he had; or maybe he had difficulties with external factors in his life – for example, maybe his dog just died.

Your filters were developed and put it place from things such as your family when you were growing up, your spiritual practice, any beliefs or values you hold from your country of origin, as well as any assumptions you've made about the world. If you don't like your current filters, beliefs or habits then you are the only person who has the power to change it.

First you must become consciously aware of what they are attracting or detracting in your life. These are your perceptions of how you see the world, and it drives your emotions and your behaviors for how you respond to the world. This is your unique reality. If you want to get different results from your reality, NLP is about changing these beliefs.

Cause And Effect

Many of us live our lives in effect – meaning that we blame others or circumstances for our bad moods and depend on others to feel good about ourselves. For example you might think, "If my spouse only understood me better, I'd be happier." Well, you are the only one who can change that. Your spouse may not even know how you feel, or you may be resisting because you might be assuming that he doesn't care. If you continue to wait, nothing will change.

If you choose to be at cause, then you are making decisions and creating what you want in life. You are not relying on others for your happiness and you understand that. While you can be supportive and cheer others to keep moving forward, you cannot take responsibility for others' emotional states - doing so places a huge weight on your shoulders that can feel quite draining. With cause, you are taking responsibility for your actions – both the good and the bad. You know that you have choices and that the world is filled with opportunities to achieve what you *really* want (Ellerton, 2006).

Failing Is The Best Feedback

Everyone will fail or make mistakes here and there. However, the thing that separates us is how we perceive it or how much we allow it to either positively or negatively affect us. In NLP, it is believed that there is no such thing as failure, just feedback. If something doesn't go as planned, it doesn't mean that you are a failure, it simply means that you've found something that doesn't work for you. It gives you an opportunity to learn how to improve and do better for next time. What if you were to view every failure as feedback?

The Body, The Mind, and NLP

❧

"*What's going on in the inside shows on the outside.*" - Earl Nightingale

We are always communicating whether it be with words, tone of voice, facial expressions, our posture, hand position, or choosing not to respond to a text message or email. When we first meet someone, we observe the body movements before speaking. We are currently sizing up each other, trying to figure out our personalities even before the first word.

As cliché as it may sound, actions speak louder than words. Research has found it takes 4 minutes to make a first impression. You only have that short amount of time to make a good impression. Surprisingly, we do not use words that much in creating that crucial first impression. Humans judge 55% based on body language. Paralanguage (manner of speaking) is accounted for 38% and the content from our words is a mere 7%. Even our voice tone and rhythm is more important than what we actually say.

Understanding How Our Mind Works

Before we discuss the different body languages, we will briefly tackle how our brain is wired. The brain has two hemispheres. The left hemisphere of our mind is in charge of the logical data processing. It is the center of conscious thinking. Compared to the right, emotions are triggered by activity in this area. The right is also responsible for our intuition and creativity.

Since we are cross-wired, our right hemisphere controls the left side of our body, while the left brain controls the right side. It follows that any body language shown on any particular side corresponds to the brain hemisphere activating it. Any action done on the left side of the body connotes conscious actions, while the right side means unconscious actions(Bandler, 1993).

Facial Language

Facial expressions are the first things we see in a person. Our moods can be quickly read depending on how relaxed or tensed our facial muscles are. Even our eyelids are powerful means of communication.

- **Smiling**

We can easily read feelings using the mouth as a

reference. A smile is associated with happiness and interest. Although smiling too much can hide disinterest. Exaggerated smiling gives assurance or courtesy to the speaker that we are listening even if, in reality, we are not. A frown gives signs of sadness and dissatisfaction. Frowning is unlikely when people first meet, for we would rather hide our true sentiments than be rude. A straight expression indicates seriousness and neutrality. Think about what impression you want to give off next time you're speaking.

- **Chin**

SENTIMENTS CAN ALSO BE SEEN BY CHECKING HOW WE USE our chin. Chin stroking is a sign of careful studying of data presented. People also perceive this as a gesture of skepticism. On the other hand, scratching connotes confusion.

- **Nostrils and Jaw**

NOSTRILS INDICATE TEMPERAMENT OR MOOD. HEAVY breathing and flaring nostrils are signs of anger. It is important to be aware of these signs. Approach these people in a soft and approachable tone. Don't force them to open up. Instead, allow them space for a few moments before engaging again.

ANOTHER INDICATOR OF TEMPERAMENT ARE THE JAW

muscles. The jaw usually goes in sync with the nostrils. Impatience and anger are signified by the flexing and pumping of the jaw muscles.

Eyes don't lie

Although eye expressions are part of facial nonverbal communication, they must be discussed in-depth.

Ophthalmics, the communication shown by eye movements, is effective tools to detect mood or sentiments(Corballis, 2012). We are sometimes oblivious to the fact that eyes let out a lot of information.

- White areas showing below the iris (the colored part of the eye) reveal the amount of stress being experienced by a person. White areas on the left eye reveal that there is stress in the right hemisphere. This means that the subject might be under stress from the body such as lack of sleep or food.

The right eye indicates stress from an external source. If white areas underneath the iris show after being exposed to stressful concepts like deadlines and overtime, the person might be receiving discomfort from those.

- Eyelids show the optimism of people. Watch the bottom lid to see the reaction of the person to your words. If the bottom lid is straight, the person is skeptical. Gaining the trust of person will soon make the lid become rounded. This means that the subject is opening up to you and that rapport is established.

THE ARMS AND HANDS

AS WE GO DOWN THE BODY, WE BEGIN TO READ MORE about what a person feels. The hands are the primary tool of humans thus we subconsciously use it to express our mood. These appendages contain more nerves connected to the brain compared to any body part.

- The hands can show anxiety, restraint or shyness if they are held together. This happens because the energy is being contained in between them. Hence, this is a way to channel negative energy such as anger and nervousness.

- If formed in a triangle shape, the hands exhibit a trait of confidence or deep thinking. A variation of this is a rhombus shape when the thumbs are extended further towards the person. A popular figure that uses this gesture is German Chancellor Angela Merkel. The hand gesture has been named the Merkel rhombus that creates a calm yet serious aura.

- Raising your arms while opening your palms will exhibit honesty and acceptance. The opposite implies defiance.

- When people show a contemplative look while using their hands to cover their mouths, they have ideas yet would rather keep it to themselves for now. Encourage people with this look to share their thoughts, for it might be able make the conversation more wholesome.

- The manner of how we cross arms also displays our confidence. A partial crossing of the arms is way for people to unconsciously soothe their nerves. People showing this behavior are feeling anxious. You can ease the mood by telling them jokes or making them laugh.

- Fully crossed arms show unwillingness to work and cooperate. If they are holding each other it is an attempt to reserve one's internal feelings.

Foot Communication

The feet are often ignored in reading body language. On the contrary, the feet are more candid than any body gestures. When people lie, they try to hide the evidence by altering their body movements, they focus on other features like the face not realizing that their feet are a dead giveaway.

By observing how we sit, we can infer whether the person is either dominant or submissive. Men usually want to be viewed as dominant, that's why they take a lot of space when sitting. They either sit in a figure four position or spread their legs apart. Women are more reserved, thus they cross their legs to confine the least possible space.

The legs also reveal the sincerity of a person while listening. When people are interested listening, their legs point towards the person's direction with the feet off slightly in a 45 degree angle. However, if the legs are pointing towards the exit this implies that the person is no longer interested in what you're saying. Be aware of the direction of your feet when communicating.

Reading peoples' body languages can help us decide how to approach the person in the friendliest and most approachable way.

Change Your Emotions with NLP

We have all experienced staring at the loads of work in front of us and feeling overwhelmed and lazy. We just couldn't get that kick start to get our minds moving. The problem is, we usually associate our workload as a boring matter. Because of this association, our body responds by slowing our actions and inducing a sleep-like state. We lose motivation and we end up opening another internet tab to use social media. The work just piles up and we lose all hope.

Another situation is during a public show. When we are faced with an audience that is looking at us, we get anxious. Following our brain, the body reacts similarly with fast shallow breaths and shaking legs. If this feeling carries on towards the performance, you might end up choking, as our emotions are completely controlling our body.

We can change our bodies' responses by shifting our emotions associated with work. Thus, we can become more productive. The technique used in this chapter is called anchoring. It is a method of recalling previous positive experiences and associating it with the current situation (Dilts, 1980).

Anchoring

Anchoring can be applied in many situations for example: at work or before and during a presentation; the moments before and during a job interview, performing on stage, meeting someone new or asking someone out on a date. It can be likened to copying and pasting positive emotions as needed. In the process, we delete the negative feelings. You can do anchoring when you wake up, on your way to work or minutes before you perform.

1. **Mental preparation**

First find a quiet place. In this technique, peace and serenity are key. Therefore, distractions need to be eliminated to maximize the effects of your mental exercises. Relax so that your heartbeat slows down and breathe deep. Cancel your outer world by closing your eyes and focusing.

1. **Recall a positive experience**

It can be anything, as long as this experience makes you feel good whenever you think of it. The memory might be when you first asked someone out on a date and the person happily accepted; or when you presented a report to your boss and got a positive response. Devote at least 10 seconds in remembering the details.

Humans are more effective if all 5 senses are activated. Let the mental pictures flow, and include the sounds and touches that were around. Do your best to relive what it actually felt like in that exact moment.

- What were the sounds around you?

- How did you feel?
- How did it smell?
- Where were you?
- What did it look like?
- Who else was around you?

1. **Associating with an action**

Keep the memory playing in your mind. While you are doing this, do an action. The most common action is slightly squeezing the index and thumb of the right hand. As you do the action, amplify the feelings flowing through you. Make the pictures more alive and vivid.

What we just did is called laying the anchor. When we recalled the event, we used our neurological components that cause an emotion to surface. The emotion has a name like happiness or sadness. This is the linguistics component at work.

Linguistics, in this context, refers to our encoding and processing of a certain memory, which is not limited to just words. We further used the linguistics part by squeezing our fingers. The action creates a virtual bookmark in our minds. Now, our brains associate every squeeze of our fingers to a happy memory. Our reaction to the memory is our programming.

1. **Repeat**

Take a few minutes and do the action at least five more times. Make sure that your mind quickly associates the action with the happy memory you just anchored. With enough practice, a squeeze will quickly flash an image of happiness in your mind.

1. **Using the anchor**

Before your performance or activity, you can invoke the anchor to give you enough confidence to feel good and do well. When you use an anchor amplify the feelings and then quickly break state when the memories are at their peak to maximize your performance. Cutting off the anchor moments before the peak will let the energy stay. Now open your eyes and you'll feel a surge of positive vibes.

You can break state by doing something different such as reading text messages or just looking at random objects around you.

Controlling your emotions by collapsing anchors

Another application of anchoring is replacing negative emotions to positive ones. This is made possible by intentionally anchoring a negative memory and a positive memory and then activating them both at the same time. At the end, the positive memory outweighs the negative one. Keep in mind, the more you practice, the more successful you'll become at this. This technique requires quite a bit of practice to master.

1. **Anchor the negative memory**

Like normal anchoring, just recall a vivid negative experience. Make it real but not too overpowering or exaggerated, for it can make things worse. Use a gesture on the left hand to lay the anchor. Recall the anchor a few times just to make sure that you feel a negative state. Finally, break state for 30 seconds.

1. **Use a positive anchor**

Next, remember an experience that made you feel the

opposite of the negative anchor. This is where you need to focus. Amplify the memory again. Meditate on the memory for another 30 seconds. Be sure to remember everything that happened. It is recommended to use an action on the right hand.

1. **Test the positive anchor**

Whenever you do the action that recalls the positive anchor, make the mental picture balloon up. The feelings that correspond to this moment should also intensify. Let go of everything and allow the feelings to swallow you up. Repeat this step 2-3 times then break state again for 30 seconds.

1. **Collapsing the anchors**

This is the tricky part and will require practice. Keep in mind that the positive anchor must be more intense than the negative one. Breathe deep and relax. Once you are ready, activate both anchors at the same time. Don't worry if it feels weird at first, because your brain is just not used to feeling two contrasting emotions at the same time. Since the positive anchor is more intense, it will overpower the negative one and thus make it collapse. Once the positive state is in control, hold on to that state for another 10 seconds. Finally, open your eyes and you will feel a surge of positive energy.

Multiple states by chaining anchors

The last technique showed you how to overpower a negative state by inducing a more intense one. This technique will teach you how to invoke several states in a short time, leading to an anchor with extreme amounts of positive energy. Chaining Anchors can help if you want a surge of positive vibes taking over you, such as productivity, confidence and relaxation. It is the most difficult technique but the one with the most benefits. Preparing for this method takes roughly 15 minutes.

1. **Preparing the chain**

On piece of paper write down the current negative state you want to change. Draw an arrow to the right towards the desired outcome.

A common example is: Stage fright → confidence

Once you have both the starting point and goal, it is now time to create the intermediate anchors. There are usually 2-3 intermediate anchors in between the current and desired states. The intermediate steps are the memories that will gradually lead towards your goal.

Next, list them all in order. Here is an example of a chain:

1. Stage fright before a performance
2. I get a feeling of disappointment because I don't have the courage to be confident
3. This builds my motivation to do my best so that everyone will be proud of my performance
4. I have rid myself of stage fright and I'm now ready to go.

The first stage is when you think about your current state. In this example, moments before your performance, you experience a case of stage fright. The second step is induced to move you away from the first one. It is a reason why you don't like your current state. After this, the third step creates a positive approach to overcome your problem that leads you to the realization of your desired outcome.

If you made your own chain, be sure that as you go towards each state that there must be progression made from a negative state to a more positive one.

1. **Testing the chain**

Now, lay the anchors by associating an action to each state. A common practice in chaining is using the fingers of one hand in a row. Induce the different anchors separately. This is to test whether the anchors can also work on their own. After each test, break state by doing something unrelated to what you're doing now.

1. **Using the chain**

Finally, you are ready to try the chain. Breathe deep and relax to prepare yourself. Recall the first state and focus. When you sense that the state is reaching its peak quickly activate the succeeding state. Do this to all the stages. As you move on through the chain, make each mental picture even more vivid and alive than the last.

Once you reach the last stage, make the mental pictures as bright as you possibly can. Hold on to the feeling for at least 10 seconds or once you reach the peak. Then quickly break state for you to maintain the energy from the exercise.

Anchoring is a very quick and effective means to move away from negative states. They require at most 15 minutes and are easy to learn. The more often the anchors are used the quicker they can be applied to and positively impact your life. They are great to use before you perform or after you wake up.

Get Healthy With NLP

Using anchors to get motivated

Health programs are usually intensive and take months to finish. It's no surprise why many people quit just after a few sessions because they lose motivation. Being healthy requires sacrifices in lifestyle, and they are never easy to do.

Before getting started make sure to anchor yourself in the right mindset by using the techniques we learned in the first chapter. Some recommended states are determination, motivation and patience. You can use either the basic, collapsing or chaining anchors depending on your preference.

You can also use anchoring to remove feelings such as craving by collapsing your state of hunger with the state of being full.

Modeling excellence

In any field, we all have people that we admire and look up to. We have high regards towards them because they show exemplary skill in what they do. Each of them have their own strategies for success.

Modeling is very similar to mentoring – it's using another

person as an example for you to mimic. It involves putting yourself in the other person's shoes in order to gain insight and understand their thoughts and behaviors. After getting permission to model the person you admire, it is important to ask that person questions to identify their ways of thinking and behavior; and if you can't get in front of the person, we can use the internet (soon to be discussed).

It begins with carefully observing the subject, filtering for the strategies that they use in order to be successful (Druckman, 2004). For this exercise we will use the example of losing weight. Modeling can also be applied in a variety of situations, including training for sports, public speaking, and parenting.

Choose a subject

Using the weight loss example, think about a person that you think has an appearance similar to how you want to look. It's best to choose someone who has kept up that shape for a long time. A common subject could be athletes because they generally practice good nutrition and utilize effective weight loss programs.

1. **Watch**

Once you have a subject, research about the person. Focus on how they are able to trim down. There are a variety of internet sources like YouTube or Vimeo that you can use to search. Athletes often get interviewed on blogs and videos about their secret to keeping fit.

1. **Searching for the secret**

Observe the behavior of the subject. Take note of how the health programs are executed. Also look for certain characteristics that make the subject different from the rest.

- What type of language does he use?
- What are his beliefs?
- What does he value?
- What is his physiology?

You are finding the X factor of the person you're modeling. Reflect back and identify the defining characteristics that were present.

1. **After finding the X Factor**, organize the information in a logical way that makes sense to you so that you can mimic or model it yourself. Test it out to make sure the desired results are achieved.
2. **Repeat this everyday**, or at least a few times a week. After applying this to your life for approximately 30 days, you or people around you will begin to notice positive changes in your behavior, attitude, and your appearance.

Attract More Wealth

Attract More Wealth
"If you can imagine it, you can achieve it. If you can dream it, you can become it."

-William Arthur Ward

Wealth is a top priority for many people so we will use money as the example of what we want to attract into our lives. Money is a sign of power and influence, and it also sends an image of hard work. It cannot buy happiness; but being broke or having no money can cause much stress, worry, and unhappiness.

There is a common misunderstanding of how we get money. People often tell us that to earn money requires going through numerous obstacles. This is not true; to get money, one of the most important strategies is - the right mindset. **The Law of Attraction (LoA)** states that thinking positive thoughts can lead to those ideas becoming reality (Devilly, 2005).

Every thought releases a mental wavelength. The law of

attraction heavily relies on the assumption that there is always an interaction between people and the universe. It can be inferred that, the universe even has a consciousness. The message inside the wavelength represents our intent. Since the universe is interacting with us, it will receive the intent and also reply with the same thing. If you always wanted to have a promotion and you meditated that intent every day, the universe will most likely give you what you wanted. On the other hand, having negative or pessimistic ideas will give you unpleasant results. After all, being pessimistic creates doubt. And when we doubt, things are less likely to happen.

Napoleon Hill, the highly successful and widely recognized author said that, "Whatever the mind can conceive and believe, it can achieve." In order for the Law of Attraction to work, we need to not only think it will happen, but most importantly *believe* it will.

Here are a few steps you can implement today to make it happen:

1. Set up goals

When we meditate using LoA, our intent must be backed up with a clear and definite goal. Clearly defined outcomes make it easier to accomplish goals without feeling overwhelmed. "I want to be rich" isn't going to work. If you *do* want to get rich then creating a path or steps that will lead to that goal is far more effective. An example could be: "By Dec. 31, 2014, I will to have a startup business that will give me profit. To do so, I will dedicate three hours (4pm-7pm) every weekday working on it." This is a place to start, and of course you want to get more specific. Ask yourself: What will I specifically be working on during those hours?; and create specific deadlines to work towards your bigger goal.

Get a piece of paper and write down everything you want in your life. Narrow down this list to the most important to you.

Your goals are the heart of LoA. Do not generalize - instead be specific and create the steps to your desired outcome.

2. Changing your belief system by reframing

The biggest challenge to success is ourselves. On the back of the paper, list any limiting beliefs that might get in the way of achieving those goals(e.g. "I don't deserve it." "I'm not smart enough.", "I can never lose weight," "I can't focus on one thing for more than a minute," or "I can never get anything right."etc.) . Be honest with yourself for it is only with genuine intent that we can make things a reality.

These are our personal convictions about life...that CAN be changed or shifted. Your goals will not come true if they are clashing with your own beliefs. As much as we want to reach success, a single cloud of doubt in our ability to achieve it can block us from achieving our goal.

Read the backside of the paper you just wrote. The challenges we wrote down are beliefs. Using the technique called framing, we can alter those negative thoughts and replace them with positive ones. Your unconscious mind cannot process a negative. It first interprets the thought as neutral or positive and then with the "not" or the "negative term" it attempts to flip it around.

An example of changing a negative statement to a positive could be instead of saying, "Don't be **afraid**," say "Be **brave**." Notice the difference and impact between those two statements. If you are already doubting your belief, think of a time when you were brave because everyone has had moments in their life where they were either forced to be brave or chose to be brave. What about the first time you raised your hand to answer a question in class; or the time you introduced yourself to someone new; or the first time you asked someone out on a date. Anyway the point is that by stating what you *do* want, you increase its awareness, causing it to be more likely to happen.

To frame, you must first close your eyes and visualize yourself. Imagine yourself in a movie. You are the director and you dictate what happens in it. Think about your limitations or negative beliefs and then reverse them. For example, "I can't lose weight," becomes "I CAN lose weight." ; or "I can't do anything right," becomes "I CAN do things right." Next you must apply that belief in the "movie". Actually, see yourself doing it and defying your own limiting beliefs. Play the movie as long as you want. You've just showed your mind that you can do better. Open your eyes and tell yourself that you can replicate what you saw in the mental movie.

Mentally playing the response you want in your mind will significantly increase the chances of it happening. Framing is useful in creating an alternative reality and then applying it in your own life.

3. Meditate

Once you've framed yourself as being successful at what it is you want in life, then you genuinely believe you can achieve it – whether it's overcoming limiting beliefs or achieving goals.

Every morning go to a quiet area, sit down, and take a five to ten minutes to think about your specific goal and what you can do to get closer to it today. You can opt to use soft music to help you get into the right mood, or use a mantra to get you in a relaxed state of mind. Visualize money being around you. Motivate yourself to be productive and positive.

When we use LoA, we feel more confident that the goals we want are what we genuinely want. Your goals will also not come true the next day, it takes patience, determination, and consistent action for you to achieve them.

NLP in Business

Meta Programs and Chunking

Meta Programs and Chunking can be highly effective in business settings. They are essentially filters that determine how you view the world around you, and have a huge impact on your behavior and how you communicate with others. The Meta Model is effective and helpful when attempting to understand another person's' perspectives of the world – his beliefs, limiting beliefs, and choices (Corballis, 2012).

In NLP, you can either chunk up or chunk down. If you chunk up, you are looking at the bigger picture. Examples of questions to chunk up would be: "What is this a part of?" "What's the bottom line?" "What is the intention behind all this?".

Chunking down is taking something and looking at it from a detailed or more specific perspective. Examples of chunking down questions could be: "If I were to cut this situation into slices, what would it look like?", "What are the specifics of this situation?" "Can you give me an example?"

It is helpful in business settings and for negotiation purposes to either chunk up or chunk down until you and the other party can come to an agreement. This system allows each of you to come to a mutual understanding and bring in perspective shifts to match each others' level.

Just as with anything in this book, Meta-Programs and Chunking takes consistent practice, and can be highly effective once mastered.

Accelerated Learning

Learning takes place beyond the four corners of the school. Even after graduating, employees are continuously bombarded with loads of information that they have to read through. Especially in a competitive market, products and new technology elevate the playing field. These new innovations can alter your performance both as a business or an employee. Learning new techniques will be easier if you apply accelerated learning strategies.

By using key concepts tied to NLP, accelerated learning strategies further maximizes the brain's potential to receive, process and recall information in a snap.

Integrating accelerated learning in your business gives you numerous benefits. Compared to conventional training methods for new employees, accelerated training courses reduce training costs and length. It is even more effective in delivering information because courses under accelerated learning are learner centered.

Aside from improving the capability of new employees, accelerated learning can also be augmented in the workplace especially during meetings. Business meetings revolve around discussing heavy matter and a ton of information.

Often times, employees become detached from the discussion when saturated with information, thus making the meetings unproductive. By using accelerated learning strategies, big information is effectively brought to the employees in bite size pieces. Furthermore, these techniques arouse the interests of participants and hence activities become interactive.

Representational systems

Each person sees the world through the five sense: sight, hearing, touch, smell and taste. We use these senses to learn from walking to running. People learn most effectively when all senses are being stimulated, and their preferred sense is targeted.

Furthermore, each person has a preferred learning method or representational system. In education, we have three main types of learners: visual, auditory and kinesthetic. Visual learners prefer reading content off books and handouts. Auditory learners would rather sit down and listen to the discussion. While kinesthetic learners like hands-on activities.

Here is a quick test to assess your learner type:

LEARNER TYPE TEST

Choose the characteristic that best suits you

Classroom behavior – do you prefer

a.) Listening to the facilitator

b.) Reading books and modules

c.) learn through hands-on activities

Speaking behavior – Do you

a.) Speak a lot

b.) Speak seldom

c.) Speak with a lot of gestures

Memory recall – Do you

a.) Remember what was discussed

b.) Remember the visual aids

c.) Remember the physical experiences

Most likely, if you answered:

- A in all questions, you are an auditory learner;

- B if you are a visual learner;
- C if you are a kinesthetic learner

Speech Patterns

Checking speech patterns are also effective ways to see a person's learning type. Engage with people and observe carefully the words they use. Watch out for clues that imply their learner type. Certain phrases like "I see your point" indicate a visual learner. "This rings a bell" are signs of an auditory learner. "I think I got it," indicates a kinesthetic learner. These speaking patterns are also useful in finding out other people's learning type so you can adjust to their language so you can connect easier and more effectively.

Visual learners primarily use words like "look", "see," "reveal", "clear", etc.; Auditory learners primarily use words like "listen", "harmonize", "tell", "squeak", etc.; whereas Kinesthetic learners will use words like "solid", "grasp", "catch on", "tap into", etc. Often times our senses overlap, but we each have a primary one we will prefer when it comes to learning and understanding the world(Masters, 1991).

Understanding how our mind works will make you realize how important it is to properly deliver information. The presentation of matter will decide whether a person will be receptive to it or not.

Eye Accessing Cues

When a person is speaking, you can use their eye movements to help determine whether a person is thinking using pictures, feelings, or sounds. This provides you with information on what their preferred learning style is.

The eyes will generally move left or right depending on what the subject's dominant side is. For example, if the person is right handed and he is recalling a memory, he will look to the left; and if he is creating something new or telling a lie, he will look to the right. If a person is describing something she's seen or imagining something new, she will look upward; if she is recalling something she's heard or creating something new, she will look laterally or to the side; if she is recalling how it felt or imagining how it would feel, she will look down (Bandler, 1975).

One way to start practicing could be observing people communicate inside a coffee shop; or watching characters on TV. Also, keep in mind that this is not always 100% correct, so if a person is right handed and he's looking up and to the right, don't *always* assume that he is telling a lie.

Setting the mood for learning

The venue of the activity plays a role in how receptive the person is to the information. According to research, facilitators must subliminally suggest the learning type of the participants to get into the mood of learning.

In trainings for new employees, a good way to do this is by setting up posters and images that give the trainees a quick preview of things they are going to discuss. Also, giving a room light and color induces positive responses from the subjects. The mind needs to be stimulated in order for it to receive information quickly.

In boardroom meetings, you can lighten up the mood by removing all clutter or unnecessary objects that distract from what's important. Architects concluded that even the space of a boardroom can affect creativity. They recommend having a room that has light and plenty of space because it creates an atmosphere of freedom for the mind to learn. A small cramped space, however, boxes the mind in and creates a feeling of being enclosed, thus, making the participants uncomfortable.

Becoming a good facilitator

Facilitators must not only be knowledgeable about the subject matter, they must also be approachable and positive. Being intimidating isn't healthy for a team to grow. A facilitator that lets each person speak his or her thoughts creates an environment conducive to learning. Other than that, facilitators need to be supportive. Positive reinforcement by encouraging a hesitant person to share their sentiments can improve the discussion. Usually, people who have ideas that are good have second thoughts before sharing it.

Afterword

As you can see, Neuro-Linguistic Programming can be beneficial in a variety of settings – from self-improvement to relationships to business settings and everyday-life. Of course, the techniques learned in this book take practice so I encourage you to review this book until you fully understand and can implement them into your life.

www.ingramcontent.com/pod-product-compliance
Lightning Source LLC
Chambersburg PA
CBHW070037040426
42333CB00040B/1705